Your Life
Your Business

How to structure your mindset for greatness

PATRICK ALEXANDER OSMAN

YOUR LIFE YOUR BUSINESS

Copyright © 2017 Patrick Osman Incorporated
Publisher: Createspace Independent Publishing Platform; 1 edition (January 19, 2017)
Graphic Designer: Karl Ibrahim

All rights reserved. No part of this book may be reproduced or transmitted in any form of by any means, electronic or mechanical, including photocopying, recording, or by any information storage or retrieval system, without written permission from Patrick Osman.

ISBN: 9781542645379

Dedication:

This book was inspired by the love I have for my family. For everything that you guys have done for me, it is an absolute honor to release this book and dedicate it to you three.

To Mum (Pauline Osman):
Mum, out of everyone in the family, throughout my whole career – it is you that has always emphasized on one thing and that is faith in God. You've raised Andrew & I to always leave everything in Gods hands and I can confidently say that Jesus has given me the strength to make it to where I am today.
Thank you Mum

To Dad (Anwar Osman):
Dad, you're the king of our home and many times throughout my career I have stopped and considered giving up, however just the thought of you has made me keep going. You generate the strength in me to do big things and I will consistently do that. When I was 19, you said to me that you want me to have a business up and running by the age of 25 and I have achieved your request. I owe you the world in return for the lessons you have taught me.
Thank you Dad

To My Brother (Andrew Osman):
Bro, you've showed me what hard work is. Growing up all my life, you've looked at Dad and saw what he has provided for our home and you've duplicated the same efforts throughout your life, which has been like a domino effect onto my career as I have implemented the same attitude as you guys. I appreciate your hard work, efforts & contributions to the family's success.
Thank you Brother

CONTENTS

	PREFACE	6
	INTRODUCTION	10
1	4 BUSINESS FUNCTIONS	17
2	BUSINESS FUNCTIONS IN YOUR LIFE	21
3	MANAGING YOUR BUSINESS EFFECTIVELY	30
4	MANAGING RISK IN YOUR BUSINESS	102
	FINAL MESSAGE	146

You and I are now a team. Contact me at any point if you need assistance:

Email: Patrick@patrickosman.com

Facebook: Patrick Osman

Youtube: Patrick Osman

Instagram: thepatrickosman

Snapchat: pattawesom

Twitter: thepatrickosman

PREFACE

Isn't it funny that in today's society, we are born into the world and we have to actually be slaves to the world? Well, that's what's portrayed to us. However, the choice of becoming something is in our control. It all comes down to our surroundings. What and who we surround ourselves with pretty much can be the answer as to where, and why you are where you are today.

My name is Patrick Osman. I am 24 years old and can confidently thank God for giving me the confidence to write this book. Like all of us, I have a story that needs to be shared with the world - but that's not why you have picked up this book. You have picked up this book because this book can appeal to YOUR life. But just to build some credibility, I am an international sales trainer and motivational speaker. I have managed sales divisions in various companies ranging from training institutions to the stock market. I am a closing machine and I have driven sales floors to points higher than Mount Everest.

I currently have a half completed university degree and am writing this book to prove to people that the old school process of going to school, getting a formal education, graduating from university and getting a secure comfortable job is the reason why in today's society,, half the world is still struggling. I'm not saying that I am against going to university because I'm probably going to go back simply because I love learning ... however, to succeed in this day and age? It's NOT the only way.

All of us have a dream and all of us have a reason as to why we have been put on this Earth. What I want you to do is: I want you to have the confidence to do what it is that you want. I don't want you to be waking up in the mornings and going to a job that you don't want to be at. So many of us hate Mondays because of the job that we are in – whereas if you were going on a holiday to some place you have always dreamed of going to and your flight happened to be on a Monday, I bet you would thank God for that specific Monday. One of my favorite quotes of all time is a famous German poet, Charles Bukowski. He said:

"How in the hell could a man enjoy being awakened at 6:30 am

by an alarm clock, leap out of bed, dress, force-feed, shit, piss, brush teeth and hair and fight traffic to get to a place where essentially you made lots of money for somebody else and were asked to be grateful for the opportunity to do so?"

That was said in 1975. The world has changed but the people in it are still being followers, hence why the middle-class is staying where they are. Everyone has fire left in them, but you need to hit a level where you are just completely sick of your life and you have to go through tough experiences to finally do a U-turn and realize the right way.

I would like to thank my father, Anwar Osman for assisting me all my life and being an inspiration for my brother and myself and funding me for the all the business opportunities I've attempted to start – which I did fail many times – but it got me to where I am today where I started in my office at home, relaying my mind onto a keyboard.

I'd also like to thank the internationally recognized personality, four-time New York Times best selling author, speaker, entrepreneur and social media freaking genius Gary Vaynerchuk, Author, Speaker & a life game changer – Author of 5 books, one of them being 'Start With Why" which I could confidently say,

- Led me to where I am today, Mr. Simon Sinek. The infamous Les Brown, throughout my whole journey – For the last 5 years, this man has been talking to me directly through my speakers and has definitely been a prime reason that explains why I am where I am today. My previous sales managers I have had in the past have also assisted me in my growth including; Rabbi Ahmed, Richard Bell & Dean Tomich. All of these figure heads have assisted me to have the drive that I do – which has saved me from the Middle Class.

This book is going to change your life. It will also change your perspective on every aspect of your life.

If it doesn't, contact me (patrick@patrickosman.com) and I will give you a personal refund. But YOU control external thoughts. YOU choose what your eyes see or your ears hear and this book being one of them.

Enjoy.

INTRODUCTION

Alright so, basically we all want to succeed right? We listen to motivational speakers and people of influence or people we look up to so we can apply their methods to try and succeed in our own personal lives. Little do we know that what we have surrounded ourselves with are all ideas and concepts that influence and impact on where we are today. Our surroundings impact upon on our decisions. Our surroundings give us a specific thought process and mentality. If you think about it, we are all human beings that have been randomly placed on a planet in the universe called Earth. We have all been given one life and it's entirely up to our decisions that will determine what will happen tomorrow.

What I have here is a concept that I'm going to share with you. I've developed this concept and it works because I have implemented this concept in my life and it brought, and continues to bring personal success throughout my business, personal and spiritual life.

You look at large corporations and businesses in today's society and they only recruit and hire the best of the best person or persons that are 'the right fit for the position.' Why? They do that to maximize the best out of people to benefit their business. Now, how about if you were to look at your life like that? How about if you were to run your life as a business? Have you ever thought of that?

Every business has 4 functions: Operations, Accounting & Finance, Marketing and Human Resources. I will explain in thorough detail in the next chapter and further on, how these functions can relate to you in your life.

Enjoy the read and congratulations on picking up this book! I really hope I can meet you one day and you can tell me about the changes that have happened in your life by implementing these simple, yet effective strategies.

The most important part of this book

Understanding who you are is a vital step in your life and this is something we are not taught in school. Had we gotten taught this in school…then we probably all would have been multi-millionaires by now and so successful! But unfortunately, we have not been taught the concept that I'm about to share with you. Once you understand this, you will be baffled as to how much power you have within you. The smartest and most accurate question that we all have raised to ourselves in class and to our friends in school is 'when are we going to use this?' And it's true! I mean, yes I understand Pythagoras theorem, but the last time I used it was in my year 9 exam. Does it apply to an engineer? Yes. Does it apply to me Being a Sales Trainer & Speaker? Hell no. Depending on your career path, you will determine whether specific subjects appeal to you or not.

We have not been taught the life skills that we need to make something out of ourselves. Allow me to teach you everything you need to have, that will allow you to have the perfect perspective towards living an abundant life. It all starts within you. You have probably heard that statement before, right? I'm about to break it down for you. When I say it starts within you, I mean it starts within your soul. You consist of three components; your soul, your mind & your body. Now the process in which we make decisions takes place within our brain. Our brain is the ultimate mastermind of our lives as it delegates tasks to our body. Our reason .. our why? Ultimately, it is happiness. The reason why it's happiness? Because that's the way we human beings conclusively want to feel throughout our lives. But where does the want or desire to feel happy generate from? It generates from our soul. Our soul delegates the feeling that we want to feel. Our brain then develops a strategy on how to achieve that feeling. Our brain then delegates the action for our body to partake in to achieve that abundant feeling. However, there is a twist to the whole story. Previous studies have shown us that our brain operates on a subconscious level 95-99% of the time and only 1-5% on a conscious level. Now, I want you to stop and think for a second. Your conscious mind is the creative side of the brain that is open to learning new ideas and concepts whereas your subconscious mind is like an enclosed box that all the leftover information that your conscious mind has processed gets stored into. Now that you understand this concept, you need to leverage off that and attempt to change your paradigm. Woah, what's that?

A paradigm is a multitude of habits and our paradigms are developed at a young age through specific life experiences which then make us who we are today. So think about your perspective towards life. Do you genuinely think that you cannot succeed? Do you genuinely not believe in yourself? Do you feel that owning your own empire one day is impossible? Or owning your own airplane is impossible?

If you do, that's fine. That's not your fault - society can consist of a lot of negative influences and can confidently provide those negative influences to us subconsciously throughout all our lives. This is why we think the way we think today. Our upbringing and our surroundings have generated the perspective and paradigm that we have towards life.

One quick perspective I'll throw at you is this ...
You can have your own plane and you can have your own empire. Understand that money is delivered to you in numbers. Luxurious items have a price to them; I'm sure we all understand that. Now, simply put a goal together and calculate what you need to bring in every day/week/month to achieve what it is you want

to achieve. Throughout the Accounting and Finance chapter, I'll explain the perfect perspective towards money and allow you to understand how to make it work for you.

However, allow me to sum it up quickly. If you're looking forward to next week's pay cheque, you are living life the wrong way. Immediately you are selling yourself and telling yourself that is your maximum financial ability and that is all you're worth. Money is everlasting. Quantitative easing will always be an option for all economies; mints will always be printing cash. Understand that you don't have to just earn your $600-1000/week. Your money is out there, go out into the world, find out who has yours and go get it!

If you stop and have a think about your life, there are specific factors in your life in which you are 100% certain on. For example, I love McDonalds. I personally really enjoy a cheeseburger and nuggets! But the reason why? Because ever since my younger age I would always really enjoy opening the brown bag, having that Mcdonald's smell of melted cheese and golden French fries rush up my nose prior to me even opening and unwrapping my food! The sound of the yellow paper being unwrapped and just knowing that it's only going to be in a matter of moments that I will be consuming one of the greatest tasting burgers of all time, one second can I get started on the crispy chicken nuggets. No... let's not do that, haha, now that's embedded in my paradigm, I actually still get the same feeling today! Not that I eat McDonalds every day! No way, however, I do believe in providing your body with what it desires on a frequent basis.

This book, Your Life, Your Business will show you a different perspective towards life and what I will attempt to do is shift your paradigm so that you too can look at life with a strategic yet positive outlook.

CHAPTER 1

4 BUSINESS FUNCTIONS

These 4 functions are interdependent towards each other which means that these functions are all mutually relying on each other.

What are the 4 functions of a business? Let's explain it nice and simple:

I) Operations
The Operations sector of a business is the sector in which the product is manufactured or the service is provided to clientele. So pretty much, transforming resources (input) into goods or services (output) that will be sold (whether it be a product or a service) for a profit.

If it is an actual product being manufactured, then the operations for that product consist of the manufacturing process and collaboration of a mix of raw materials to which would lead to the final manufactured product.

If it is a service, the service being provided is to the client.

II) Human Resources
Human Resources, this is the fun one! The function that relies on mankind to run the company or business. Human Resources is the function that consists of the management of all employees of the organization or business. In this function, an organization needs to recruit the most suitable individual for the position to assure that efficiency and effectiveness is achieved within that position. If not, that specific employee position may be terminated

III) Marketing
The marketing sector of the business is the sector in which the business attempts to advertise its products or services to its market through various marketing methods including media (radio, TV, internet, social

media), billboards, signage, pamphlets etc. in an attempt to generate and increase sales revenue.

Marketing notifies society about products and services however, depending on the business or companies, consumer perception will determine whether prospects will buy or not (Remember this part, I'm coming back to this later on)

IV) Accounting & Finance

Accounting and Finance is the function that the three other functions work hard for to ensure this area is satisfied. It's one of the most important, if not the most important function. Why? Without this one, you can't pay for anything! Including stock, employees or anything for the business. This function in any organization needs to always be in profit, opposed to deficit. After all the hard work that you put in through hiring the right employees, manufacturing and marketing the products, you want all the steps to be right in the first place to make sure prospects turn into clients, and then make sure that they are retained. The more income invested into the company, the higher and quicker the chance of expansion. But the capital needs to be invested into the right areas to assure that the company is steering in the right direction. I mean, imagine driving a car from one side of the country and you're wanting to get to the other side and you end up North instead of East or South or West!... Woops! You don't want that! So companies need to financially plan properly what they are doing with their funds instead of misplacing them or spending instead of investing.

CHAPTER 2

BUSINESS FUNCTIONS IN YOUR LIFE

I) What is Operations in your life?
In a company, the Operations sector is where the company manufactures its product or provides its service to sell as output, right?

So what is the Operations sector in your life?

YOU! You are your own product! Your mind, body and soul are your components that God has manufactured and composed to be you. Now with those components you need to make sure you're purchasing the best raw materials from the right suppliers; so, who are the suppliers in your life?

The suppliers are the influencing factors that assist the growth of your mind, body and soul.

The correct suppliers to work alongside;

Mind – Knowledge, education, work experience, effective utilization of time (suppliers)
Body – Fitness, effective health, correct nutrition (suppliers)
Soul –family time, having a set of ethics and morals, abiding by your religion or a form of ethics and also listening to what your soul wants and forcing your mind and body to give your soul its desires. (suppliers)

Who are the INCORRECT suppliers to work alongside?

Mind – Wasting time by playing games (when the money could be made or knowledge or experience could have been gained), gambling, sleeping while the economy is spinning, watching movies and any other substance that can take your attention away from your success and prosperity.

Body – Smoking, taking drugs, unhealthy nutrition, unhealthy sleeping patterns

Soul – Not having a sense of morals or ethics – which will not give yourself any form of a boundary or barrier to making sure you don't breach in your life, which could lead to you delving your hands in the unethical business.

Your job is to make sure you manufacture the best product to sell in today's marketplace and to make sure that you are in demand in today's society.

How can you achieve this?

Consistently making sure that your goal is to become a powerhouse in every sector of your life! Being a person who has an education (doesn't necessarily mean a formal education) and feeds their mind consistently with knowledge and information that one did not know the day before, attending the gym every day and assuring the blood flow to your brain and throughout your body is working at its best. Most importantly, being close to your religion, whether it be Christianity, Judaism, Islam, Buddhism, Hinduism etc. By being close to your religion, it gives you a set code of ethics which gives you your do's and don'ts in life (Quick note: Our religion influences our soul, our soul influences our mind, the mind then influences the body.)

Now, just like the food market, McDonald's has the best product and everyone purchases it because it tastes the greatest (according to the success of the business.) Your goal is to make sure that every company would want to hire you or everyone will want to buy your product because of you! Because you are your own product and if you were a CEO of a large organization, who would you hire? Nothing but the best right?

One who is highly knowledgeable in his/her field who also has work experience and a HUNGER to succeed?

Or would you hire one who isn't knowledgeable in his/her field and doesn't have work experience let alone a drive to succeed?

Life gives us these examples on a silver platter, go for a walk today in society and you will see exactly what I'm talking about. It's purely because of one's surroundings that have impacted upon their lifestyle that has led to where they are today. It's a simple formula, your surroundings (your suppliers!).

Work alongside the right suppliers – surround yourself with the right surroundings – and you will assemble a product that will be in high demand in no time.

II) What is Human Resources in your life?

You are the CEO of your life. You are the one who picks and chooses who you affiliate with, this factor in your life is the one that you don't need money to start doing properly, this one all comes down to your decisions and how you utilize the right people around you to your advantage. You know when you speak to people and they say things like I couldn't start the business because I don't have the money? I've heard that a thousand times. If you surround yourself with the right people, then you wouldn't ever be saying that as you would understand that you probably would have had the funds to start off whatever business it is that you're wanting to start.

So as the CEO of your own life, what's the right thing to do in your company? Which option has the likelihood to generate more revenue for your business? 5 unskilled employees or 2 skilled employees?

I hope you picked 2 skilled employees! Because yes that's right. That's the answer, why? As it is cost efficient as well as no training involved and they will benefit your firm. (total productivity) That is how you should think when it comes to your friends, are your friends benefiting you? Are they influencing your life for the better or for the worse?
The most intelligent book of all time is the Bible, and in the bible it states "walk with the wise and become wise, for a companion of fools suffers harm" (Proverbs 13:20).

It's not our fault, it's the way we are built. We buy what we see, we are influenced by what is around us. If you hang around with 5 millionaires every day, the language they speak will influence the language you speak. The content of which they speak about will become an interest of yours and ultimately what you want is to employ people in your life who will bring forth these conversations with you, which in turn will assist your growth.

Now, I don't want you to take this the wrong way. I'm not saying use people and then leave them, no! But what I am saying is, become friends with people who come from good families, who have ethics, morals and people who actually know where they will be in 5 years time because of their drive to succeed. If you do that, opposed spending time with a bunch of guys/girls that play games all day or a bunch of girls that just watch TV and 'keep up with the Kardashians' the Kardashians are getting paid and they ain't!

Proverbs 27:17 says that "friends should sharpen each other like iron sharpens iron"

You tell me out of those options, which one will become successful?

The best part about this specific section is that this one is all up to us, the ball is in our court.

III) What is Marketing in your life?

Alright, this one is interesting...
We will start this one with a question… When someone is on your Facebook page or someone that you know thinks about you, what do they think about? What category do they put you in? Are you considered

someone they look up to? If so, why? Or are you considered someone that they would not want to affiliate themselves with. If so, then why? It all depends on how you have marketed yourself!

We all need to think about how we are marketing ourselves, what people think of us and our reputation. Consumer perception is very important!. Our reputation on the market, if it's negative, then nobody is doing business with you! But if you have a very positive reputation then that would give you an advantage over the other individual who is not reading what you are reading right now ;). Marketing yourself and your brand is the key to success as you are ultimately notifying the world as to who you are, what you do and how you add value to the world.

IV) What is Accounting & Finance in your life?

This one is plain and simple and it explains itself. It is broken down into 4 components;

1) Investing in yourself

2) Creating Income Streams

3) Emotions & Finance

4) Return On Investment

I'll explain this in more detail later under managing your business effectively, however briefly, we are dealing with whatever cash you have in your life and putting it in the right places. Pretty much reinvesting back into yourself to become a better you. In this world, money is power, you can do a lot with it and you can buy knowledge through courses and books.

Now, I'm not saying money is everything because that debate can be potentially started right now. But, at the same time in this world, money will feed, educate, medicate and clothe your families.

CHAPTER 3

MANAGING YOUR BUSINESS EFFECTIVELY

I) Operations

Earlier, I briefly spoke about the Operations sector in your life. Now that you understand that you are a product, you need to understand that every day. Persuasion takes place in your life and consistently we are selling at all times. Whether it be a job interview that we go for or whether it be with your spouse regarding what you want to have for dinner or even merging lanes in traffic. Everything in life is considered a sale because people are consistently thinking and getting persuaded to do things in a specific way. Now whenever you go to make a decision on purchasing an item for yourself, whether it be an outfit, house, car or anything that you are going to use – you will notice that you want to get obviously the best product for yourself, whichever product is going to benefit you the most right? Well, if you want to acquire the best products for yourself, wouldn't you think that society thinks very similar to yourself?

I want you to think about this - let's use a job interview for example. You apply for a position, this company that you have applied for to potentially work for not only has your application in front of them but they have probably another 50 applications next to yours. Now logic says that the recruiters are going to select the 'most suitable' candidate right?

However what makes the 'most suitable' candidate the most suitable candidate? The answer is simple, the one who has the best product.

So let's say for example you're applying for a Sales Management position and the recruiters want to find out who you are. Are you tenacious? Are you a leader? Have you managed a sales team before? In the event that you have managed a sales team, what sort of numbers did you lead that team to bring home? What sort of education have you undertaken? What do you know about sales? Do you know about business growth? What value will you add to the company that you are applying to work for? Now, the person who confidently and correctly answers all that companies questions is going to get that position! Simple, but now that you're reading this book, you are now conscious that there is competition out there, and EVERYONE around you is your competitor. Therefore, you must dominate your market and differentiate your product. How do you differentiate your product (YOU)? Let's get into that now!

Goals

Step number 1. Before understanding anything, you need to get a solid grasp on this concept first, Goal Setting. Goal setting is a vital component in anyone's life because it gives you a sense of direction as to where you are going and what you are working towards. There's no point in waking up every morning like a deadbeat and working towards next week's pay cheque. There really is no point! I mean you are not living life. At one stage in all of our lives, I understand we need to get a job, for sure, hey I've worked with least 25 different workplaces! I've had more jobs than I have had years of existence on planet Earth! But that's because I've been busy searching for what it is that I love. And finally, I realized after years and years of hunting, that my passion is in motivational speaking and training!

The way in which you set your goals needs to be written down every morning and every night so that you are conscious of where you are going every day and what you are working towards. You need to remember when you set goals, establish the following:

1) What do you want?
2) When do you want it by?
3) Why do you want it?
4) How are you going to get it?

Once you have established exactly what it is that you want and a methodology on how you can achieve it, you then write your goals down in the present! Not in the future or in the past, you write them down every day in the present as if you have already achieved them.

For examples, my goals I write every day are written exactly like this:

I am international sales trainer and motivational speaker

My net worth is over 50 Million

I am earning $100,000/month from speaking engagements and book sales

All my books are New York's Times Best Sellers

I am building 10 new churches worldwide every month

I have a beautiful happy and healthy family

I love my partner because she is my inspiration

I am consistently inspiring people all over the world

I have endless energy and constantly produce to benefit the world

Jesus is with me throughout every step that I take

Time is a gift and I appreciate being alive

By setting your goals exactly like this, you are selling your subconscious mind that it has already happened. Now, this not only provides you with an unbelievable feeling at the time that you are writing your goals, however it will also make your brain operate on a daily basis with a positive mindset and forces you to take the required action as you are aware that you have a mission and a dream that you want to achieve.

Goal setting gives you a reason to be on planet Earth. It gives you a reason to wake up in the morning and it provides you with step by step tasks to achieve, which will lead to your growth as a person! The main reason why some of us don't make it and get what we want in life is because we don't make it our target to achieve whatever it is that we want.

Now, what happens is that people set goals and don't end up achieving them but that's because of the influence of their emotions. See, what happens is that we create whether we will make it in life or not, we create that because initially, we set that standard in our paradigm.

The diagram below simply shows why goals are not achieved:

What happens in our minds is that we think of a specific goal which is our immediate thought, then after that, our emotions will get in the way and influence the second thought which is a perspective on that goal (initial thought). The influence will have an emotional underlying asset behind it like fear for example, and immediately your emotions will want you not to pursue the achievement of that goal because they want you to be complacent in your life. Why should you change? Your emotions are happy, they are content. However, my question is, why did you have that initial thought? You had it for a reason. It's your SOUL who gave you that thought. You will find out shortly exactly how to manage your emotions when you understand the breakdown of the mind, body and soul which is coming up next.

'People who don't have goals end up working for people who do have goals'

Now that you are conscious of the fact that we as humans are broken down into 3 components, let's dive into them.

The soul, the mind and the body. Prior to me breaking this concept down into detail and showing you exactly how you are going to have the best product, (the best you) I want you to make sure that you are consistently conscious of this concept because that will put you in a position of power as you will be conscious of the human being's downsides and be able to advance a lot further than your competitors.

It's actually quite interesting how it works. It's like a little chain of command inside us which looks like this:

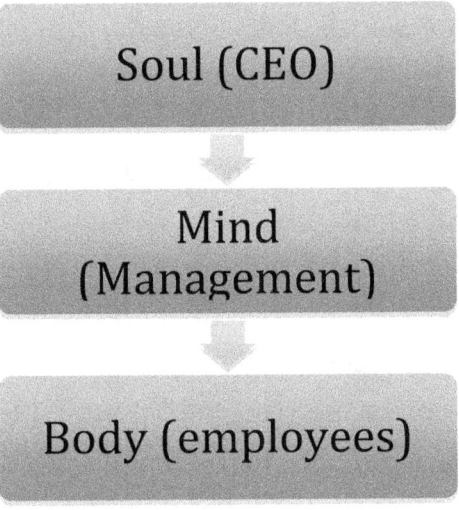

This image depicts the fact that all orders or requests inside us come from within our soul. Our soul then delegates the task to the mind to strategize, which then delegates the practical task to our body to implement into action.

1) Soul

Let's start with the soul. The soul explains why we are alive. All our wants, desires, needs, likes and anything that we are attracted to is originated from our soul. Whenever we set any form of goal, it comes from our soul. But when we don't follow through with it, it's not our soul's fault, it's our mind's fault. For example, New Year's resolutions? Have you noticed that not many people commit to actually resolving their problems? I mean at the beginning of every year, everyone is motivated, they are pumped because they feel that life has given them a fresh start for that year, so they are ready to commit to their new year's resolution and make a change, then all of a sudden, just over 90% of people go back on their word. For example, one commits to wanting to lose 15 pounds, however, they never commit to the set diet or exercise to make it happen. Why, though? They initially made the decision to WANT to lose that weight right? Why did they make that decision? The reason why, is because their soul isn't happy in the body that it's wrapped in! It wants a change! However, now that we understand that, the body is an additional component to who you are. The body wants to be lazy, it doesn't want to work, it's like a dead weight to the soul. I mean when one wakes up in the morning, our bodies don't want to leave that bed! However, if your soul is stronger than your body, then you will force your body to get up! And that's the point of difference that you now understand. So to sum that up?

You need to simply do the things that your body does not want you to do to satisfy what your soul desires.

Connecting with yourself is one of the most important attributes to do on a day to day basis. Knowing that our minds operate subconsciously (90% of the time), you need to stop for at least 10 minutes a day and connect with yourself because, consciously, daily we don't do it. And the best way to probably go about that is read the book 'The Power of Now' by Eckhart Tolle. The power of now makes you get into the now. When I say get into the now, I mean by being conscious of your subconscious mind. Showing simple gratitude towards tiny things like the Universe, the opportunity to live, your family members, your limbs!

Some people don't have the opportunity to live the life that we live and we take all this for granted because we simply don't leverage off it! People would rather spend time procrastinating and wasting time, while they have a brain that works, arms that function, legs that function. You can do SO much in this world with those abilities, however, people are too involved in the rat race to understand and realize this concept! The answer is in front of us, we just need to take action and get where we need to get to. Pay close attention to your soul and connect with yourself on a daily basis for at least 10 minutes. If you can't give yourself 10 minutes, I don't know what you are doing with your life that is more important than yourself. The best way to connect with yourself is to spend time with nature. When you spend time with nature, you will notice the little things in life, feelings the breeze of the wind hitting you or listening to the waves crash against the rocks. When our ears hear that, we feel at ease and enjoy the moment. It gives you a chance to stop and think about life and have gratitude for what you have.

Now, whenever you set a goal in your life, whether it be a personal or a career goal, your connection with your soul will allow you to achieve this specific goal. Because all goals are set from within us, our soul sets any goal that we want to achieve because it is affiliated with our wants & desires. For example, one of my goals is to build schools in countries that are suffering highly from poverty to assist the change in their lives. That goal has been set from my heart because, helping and assisting people is what makes me happy and comfortable at heart. If I don't work closely with myself and my inner soul, I will be influenced by my external surroundings and not stay focused on my goal! So always remember that your soul needs attention, you need to pay attention to yourself, which will then make you a priority in your life, because at the end of the day, YOU OWE YOU!

2) Mind

This component is the one that you have full control over; your brain is literally where everything starts getting put into play. Once you have written your goals down, realize what is your why? What is your purpose? Your brain will then develop a strategy on how to achieve exactly what it is that you want. Now, your brain establishes who you are and your body, actions and speech represent what goes on inside your mind. Therefore, you need to make sure that your brain is your ultimate powerhouse. That's why I have such a passion for learning and I highly advise that you constantly learn. Knowledge separates the ones who know from the ones who don't know and in this life you want to be the latter of the two. The more knowledge in your mind, the more you become different opposed to everyone else and you know for a fact that it's the ones that are different, that stand out. You don't want to be a consumer in society, you want to be a producer and what forms a producer is knowledge. You need to consistently learn, consistently! I stress this point with thorough emphasis.

The average CEO reads 4 to 5 books a month. Think about that, 4 to 5 books a month! Imagine how much knowledge is going into the average CEO's mind every month that we are missing out on! And their status has proved their differentiation. So what you need to do is make your mind the strongest mind out of all and the best way to do that is to put knowledge in there - that's it! With the amount of knowledge you put inside your mind, it will allow you to grow, prosper and understand whatever industry it is that you're in, properly and confidently. Your time needs to be spent very wisely. As the clock ticks, we age and as we age, we want to make sure that every moment we spend on ourselves now, we intend on it providing us with a comfortable and happy lifestyle in the coming years. The comfortable and happy lifestyle won't come if you don't work now, you need to generate experience and throw so much knowledge into your brain to get where you want to go. We are in 2017, do you know how many books that have been written in the past 2017 years? Whatever industry it is that you are in, I guarantee that there is a publication that explains qualities, skills and attributes that you could implement in your industry just from reading that one book! Imagine you read 4 to 5 books a month, how far ahead you would be opposed to other people in your industry, think about it! I want you to set yourself a target after completing this book and commit to it. Set a target where you guarantee that you will read at least 2 books a month and scale it up from there, watch what a powerhouse you are going to become.

Now, a lot of people have the same common objection that I've heard all my life, as a matter of fact, I use to be one of these people.

"But I don't like reading"

Heard that before? I have too, I would say it quite a lot

to my father when he used to advise me. There are many ways to learn; YouTube, Google, online courses, face to face courses, attending seminars and workshops, webinars and the list goes on. See, I used to be one of these people once I grew my emotional intelligence and realized that my mind doesn't want to read. However, my soul knows what's best for my mind, therefore, regardless of what my mind or body want, I'm going to read. Irrespective of any emotion, don't allow your emotions to influence any of your decisions, control yourself, be determined, strong-willed and grow yourself constantly. That's the mindset of a winner.

The reason why I emphasize on consistent learning and educating your mind, is because your mind is easily influenced. You control what goes in there, therefore it forms and solidifies your perspective towards life and you want to make sure that you stay motivated and have a positive outlook towards life. Well, let me ask you a question, do you have a shower every day? (I hope you do!) I'm sure you do right? Why do you do that? To keep your body clean right? Well, just like the human body needs to be cleaned daily, the mind needs to be cleaned daily. How do we do that? Simple. Motivation! Every day, you need to watch a daily motivation video, read a motivational post, and consistently inspire your brain to keep you on track to achieve your daily/weekly/monthly and yearly goals. Because our minds are influenced by our surroundings, you need to force your mind to be surrounded by positive vibes. I suggest that every morning you wake up, watch a motivational video to inspire you and keep you on track. Do it right before your shower, because in the shower you have nothing to do besides two things; clean your body & think. And in the shower is where you think the most, therefore if you watch a motivational video and think about your goals, that's what you'll be thinking about in your shower!

Don't forget, I spoke about suppliers earlier, you need to make sure that suppliers you're working with only benefit your business! The best suppliers are the ones that are adding value to you, not the ones taking away from you. Time is not on your side. Remember that the more you learn, the more you earn. So stay focused, have a break when your actions have proved that you deserve it too but also, stay productive at all times!

3) Body

Your body makes things happen, your body is the hands-on person who gets the tasks completed. Your feet walk you to the shower, your hands pick up the book that you need to read, your fingers type onto the keyboard, your hands and feet drive you to the places you need to go to. Now, one thing I'll say to you about the body…. it doesn't like to participate. It is lazy. It naturally doesn't like to get up from the bed. It doesn't like to go and exercise - It doesn't like doing any of these things!

A perfect example of this, you want to watch a movie. You've mentally prepared yourself that tonight, you're going to watch a movie or you're going to watch television. You've arrived home, you've had your dinner, you've had your shower, you're now in the most comfortable clothes in the world! You literally just sat down on the couch, you look for the remote and you see it on the table or on the other couch. Your body IS SO IRRITATED!! It makes you speak on its behalf and say: "oh my God, I just sat down!" You then may roll your eyes out of frustration on behalf of your body, complain a bit more, then eventually get up and retrieve the remote. See, now that you are aware of the human body's behavior, you need to address it and detach yourself from it. Complaining won't put that remote control in your hands, get up get the remote and sit back down. Don't be lazy, do not allow your body to be lazy, control it from every angle.

But we need to train the body to make it like it. Your body needs to enjoy being active. It needs to enjoy to move - it needs to enjoy to work. So how do we do that? By getting it into a habit, by training your body and getting it into a habit, it will make your body reliant on the specific movements that you put it through.

Now, I am no personal trainer, however, if you are not in a habit of exercising, you need to crack into the habit immediately. At least 1 hour a day of movement needs to happen, Meditation takes care of the soul. Knowledge takes care of the mind. Fitness and nutrition take care of the body. You need all three to be performing at their best.

Exercise

What's a dream of yours that you've always wanted to achieve?

....
....
....
....
....
....
....

Irrespective of the difficulty of achieving your goal, write down a step by step method of how you think you can achieve it

....
....
....
....
....

What have you learnt from this chapter that is going to add value to your journey of being great?

....

....

....

....

....

....

....

....

....

....

....

....

....

....

II) Human Resources

Wow! I love this function of our lives! Because this one is completely in our control. You are the CEO of your business - who you end up becoming is your product. However, if you are the CEO that means you call all the shots right? You're the boss. You say who works for your company. You say who gets fired and you say which direction the business should be heading towards, right?

Well, guess what? Right now the people who you surround yourself with every day are currently employees of your business. That's right, all your friends and all your family members and whoever you decide to associate yourself with currently work for you.

People's' words and actions are a part of your surroundings. You can't control your ears from hearing and not hearing things. If you are not deaf, then your ears will hear whatever is around you. If you are not blind, then your eyes will see whatever it is around you. Now knowing that as human beings, when it comes to learning about something or experiencing a specific moment, the only method in which we will be able to do it, is limited by our 5 senses. Knowing that the subconscious mind is like a sponge, you can't be surrounding your eyes and ears around negativity. You simply cannot be doing that, because once you surround yourself around negativity, that's going to influence the way you consciously think and it will influence your actions. See, if you are surrounding yourself with individuals who are motivating you to become a better version of you, what do you think is going to happen? Your friends will influence you to become a better you and you will listen because you've made the conscious decision to become their friend. HOWEVER on the flip side, if you were surrounding yourself with a bunch of deadbeats who do not benefit you at all and consistently take your time whilst providing no positive return or benefit towards your life. What do you think is going to happen? You'll become exactly like them. Time is against you. You can't afford to be surrounding yourself with people who are not going to benefit you. You need to make sure that your friends are people who are going to motivate you and push you.

Now I want you to stop and think for a second, who are your friends? Who are your family members? What do they say to you when you have ideas, and you've explained an idea to one of these people? It's inevitable that one of them has put you down in the past. I'm very big on family, but if I had listened to some of my non-immediate family member's advice in the past, I would probably be on a $60,000/year salary, working for a bank and wouldn't be as confident as I am today. But I knew for a fact that I was not born to be average and I have the intelligence to choose not to process the advice that was given to me from some of my non-immediate family members because with respect to their careers and life experience, they weren't eligible to give me career advice.

People will put you down. Once you notice that people within your circle are starting to put you down or starting to shun your creativity and open mind, drift away immediately. If you have an idea of creating a product or service or doing something positive with your life and someone in your circle puts you down, you need to leave that circle immediately.

I mean, if they are not a credible and successful source then clearly, they don't have the right to be giving you advice because you're both in the same boat, you are just the one with the idea. So you need to make sure your surroundings are completely positive.

There have been so many Friday & Saturday nights where I have been home alone stuck on YouTube, watching sales training videos or watching business consulting videos educating myself and growing my brain because I just wasn't interested in going out with my friends and drinking and picking up girls and all that jazz. It's never been my field - I have never enjoyed it. I would rather be a producer than a consumer and that's the mindset of an entrepreneur. So guess who my friends became? Eric Thomas, Simon Sinek, Gary Vaynerchuk, Grant Cardone, Bob Proctor, Les Brown, Tony Robbins and the list goes on with other influential figures. They were and still are my friends for a solid 2 – 3 years and till now, all from YouTube.

So while all my friends were getting drunk and hooking up with awesome good looking women, I was in taking information that they were not. Once you focus on yourself and becoming a better you, you will then attract the right people in your life.

You need to understand how to recruit the right people in your life. Now, there are 2 main topics I'm going to cover here which are, understanding who people are and gaining the right friends.

1) Understanding who people are

You need to understand who you are employing into your business. You are too busy attempting to create a lifestyle that's going to provide you with absolute abundance, therefore surrounding yourself with the wrong people is not going to get you to where you want to go.

So how do we fix that? You need to know WHO you are dealing with. Over the years working in sales management, managing sales teams and dealing with various people, I've come across so many different personalities and I've realized a few common traits between specific individuals personalities and animals. Here are my conclusions, collectively we all do have a mix of all of these traits in us, however, people can be classified primarily into 2 of these 5 of personalities:

i) LION

The lion is the king of the jungle. The lion does not have time to waste. Once the lion walks in the room, the room is suppressed with a blanket of dominance due to the distribution of authority throughout the room from the lion. The lion is commonly known to make very efficient decisions because it wants to achieve its goal. A lion has an end goal, let alone a sense of direction in front of any decision that it makes. Lions tend to be very dominant characters, with a little patience, very abrupt and direct responses come from the lion's mouth alongside a strong willed and forceful personality. The downside to a lion is that they always think they are right, in every situation which is simply an egotistically based decision.

ii) DOLPHIN

Dolphins are too cheeky, you have to watch out for these guys because they just love to have fun! They are very influential characters, but what makes them highly influential is their personalities. They are full of life, energy, optimism, spirit and put aside how outgoing they are, they just have to sell you the story and you will paint the perfect picture in your mind which will assist in persuading you to take action with them. But the downsides to a dolphin is that they make impulsive decisions and they tend to make a bucket load of impulsive decisions in a few hits, then tend to get overwhelmed because they realized they made a mistake by not analyzing and thinking about all potential scenarios. They have beautiful hearts and tend to be very caring.

iii) DEER

Deer's are very steady and patient characters with a tactful and humble attitude. They tend to embrace their comfort zone and struggle to change any situation that they are used to. Deer are very resistant to change. They are satisfied with where they are and don't need change because their lives have proved they are living in a safe environment. Fear is a deer's worst enemy. Deer cannot deal with fear, let alone think about it. Fear influences them a lot, hence why they are resistant to change and the fear of the unknown is one of the biggest no-go zones for deer. This explains why they embrace their comfort zone and struggle to adapt to changes. They are very accommodating, tend to have beautiful hearts and really embrace support and teamwork as they like seeing themselves in the same boat as other people. The downsides to a deer are their resistance to change, which won't allow them to prosper further in their lives.

iv) OWL

The patient reserved bird sits high on the single branch, lonely, but using its eyes to observe to make sure that everything is in pedantic order. The owl won't miss a beat with its reserved personality. All its decisions will be made based on an analytical thought process. Usually, individuals who graduate from university as engineers, doctors, teachers and high academics tend to be owls. The upsides to an owl is that they tend to forecast really well & don't come across much issues, however the downsides of an owl are that they can get too caught up in attempting to make everything perfect, which then prevents them from taking earlier action.

v) CAMEL

The camel is a very arrogant and ignorant individual who tends to just let life pass them, while they don't really care about their surroundings. However, when they input their perspective, it always tends to be a negative perspective, they are naysayers and always have an answer for everything and according to them, they are always right, when in reality they don't have the expertise to provide the best advice for the situation. The downsides to a camel is that, they don't have a sense of direction, they are complacent with their current situation and even if they are in a bad stage in life, they refuse to pick themselves up and move forward with any change because they lack belief. The upsides to a camel? NOTHING!

Just before I explained all the personalities, I explained that we are a mix of all of these personalities, however, primarily we are 2 of them right? Well, I'll let you know, that the second personality will only be revealed to you once a person likes or trusts you. For example, I am a lion/dolphin & whenever I meet someone, I don't show my dolphin side at all, because I need to establish authority initially so whoever I'm speaking with, knows where we both stand in any situation, whether I trust or like who that person is, is when I will determine whether I will reveal my dolphin side or not.

Knowing the 5 different personalities, now you can categorize people when you meet them, and find out what attributes and skills they have and how you can use them to your advantage to assure that you employ the right people in your life.

2) Gaining the right friends

Now if your current friends are not ones who will benefit your business, you need to address the issue right now. I want you to understand that if you need to make a life changing decision, it means you will have to leave them behind. Let them go! You don't have the time to surround yourself with people who are not going to benefit you. You will have to attempt to find a new set of friends and it's pretty easy nowadays especially with the rapid growth of social media. It really allows you to easily segment your hobbies/interests to find like-minded individuals to become friends with. Try the any of the below strategies to attempt to find/make new friends:

- Participate in face to face courses of your interest to find like-minded people

- Join online/face to face societies or clubs of an area of your interest which will lead you to like-minded people (meetup.com is PERFECT for this)

- Like pages on Facebook of your interest and speak with other bloggers online regarding whatever area it is that you're interested in and build your relationship with them.

- Volunteering in any event, whether it be a church event or a local community event - This will get you further exposure to other potential like-minded people

Attempting to find new friends outside of your current circle is difficult, I understand. Simultaneously you need to think about yourself at all times and you need to be assured that your surroundings are nothing but a benefit to you. If you meditate and speak with people that you know already have the same interest as you, that already gives you immediate rapport because you've both voluntarily made the conscious decision to be in the same room as each other due to initial common likes/hobbies/interests.

Exercise:

Pick 3 people that you currently spend most of your time with, what personalities are they?

....

....

....

....

....

....

....

Which Personality are you and why do you think so?

....
....
....
....
....

What skills would you like to adapt from other personalities and why?

....
....
....
....
....
....
....
....

....
....
....
....
....
....

What course(s) are you willing to take to find new friends?

....
....
....
....
....
....
....
....
....

....

....

....

....

....

What are online societies/social media pages you going to subscribe to, to meet new like-minded people?

....

....

....

....

....

....

....

YOUR LIFE YOUR BUSINESS

....
....
....
....
....
....

Email: Patrick@patrickosman.com

Facebook: Patrick Osman

Youtube: Patrick Osman

Instagram: thepatrickosman

Snapchat: pattawesom

Twitter: thepatrickosman

III) Marketing

When you think of a specific brand, say Coca Cola for example, what do you think? I think international, fizzy drink, successful company etc. Now when people think of you, what do they think of? Their perception of you is called consumer perception. Consumer perception is generated in 2 ways:

1) In which a brand/product is marketed
2) The quality of the actual product itself

Now my question to you is how do you market yourself? Nowadays, social media has a large stake in how people perceive us and it's funny because it's tiny things like what we post statuses about that generate people's perception of us. Whenever one posts a status, photo or video of whatever it is that you post about, people will make a comment about you in their minds which will create their perception of you. The word will spread as well - people talk. For generations people have been talking. Consider this 'word of mouth.' Whether it be good or bad content about you, people will talk about you. Always be conscious of whatever it is that you post on any form of social media, because people will categorize you in their minds. For example, whenever someone thinks of Patrick Osman, what do you think?

I've asked this question to numerous amounts of people and I've received a common answer of; motivational speaker, driven, successful, entrepreneur, business minded - It's because of how I have marketed myself. I have been consistent with my regular status updates and they have always been of very similar lines and topics which have allowed me to generate a lot of business. People know me for who I am and what I do because that's what I consistently speak about whether it's in day to day conversations with people or online.

Whatever it is that you do for a career - if people don't know what you do, it's not their fault? It's your own fault for not marketing yourself as frequently and as effectively as you should be. This is where your emotions need to be pushed aside and you need to, like Nike says 'just do it'.

Don't stop and think, 'if I speak about this topic frequently, people will get annoyed at me' or 'if I post about this topic frequently people will get annoyed at me' - this is the wrong mentality to have! If anyone does find you annoying for whatever it is that you do, you don't need them in your life. Simple. As a matter of fact, I've had many people in the past delete me from Facebook because they've found me annoying. I've seen them around in local shopping malls or local gatherings and they've approached me and told me that they have deleted me. I have been so busy that I have had no idea that they have deleted me. I'm too busy focused on my goals, on growing my business, on letting the world know who I am and what my motivational messages are. By the way, you will come across these people - which personality do you think they are? (CAMELS!)

Marketing your products and services is something that you need to do on a very frequent basis. Some examples of these avenues are, putting signage on your car, posting on social media, building relationships with other people and cross marketing, generating more leads through referrals and past clientele. Constantly marketing yourself and your products will generate the consumer perception that you are after! See the end goal is for people to associate your brand/product or service with the initial thought of you alongside positive qualities like; respectful, nice, confident, considerate, genuine. That's the category where you want to be in, you don't want to be known as the negative person who always has something negative to say, because you will deter people away from you. You want to do literally the opposite of that and attract people to you. How you do that is through marketing yourself in a correct and presentable manner.

The most efficient way to get in contact with anyone these days is through the piece of technology that we all have in our pockets, our phones! To market yourself effectively, you need to cover all forms of social media. You need to be on each and every single form of social media. Let's face reality, everyone's life revolves around their phones these days and you can reach 1000 people's pockets in less than 5 seconds with a simple post. So use social media to your advantage and get your name out there as much as possible. Your target for about 4 -5 posts a day.

So social media is an area of which you should confidently understand now so let's move onto physical presence.

According to various different studies, the average human mind generates a first impression within 5 to 10 seconds. So when you're out in public, you always need to make sure that you are ready to meet anyone and everyone. Always make sure you are well presented, dress code sorted so that if and when anyone sees you, you control their perception by having a presentable outfit, smelling nice and being well spoken. This will lead to individuals having a positive consumer perception of who you are. In any event that someone talks about you, whether it be online or face to face, you have branded yourself in an effective manner which has controlled people's perception of you and your brand.

The First Class Mentality

The first class mentality is the mentality where you, as a person accept nothing but the best in everything that you do. The first class mentality makes you go the extra mile to assure your differentiation.
With presentation and brand, you need to have the 'first-class' mentality. You need to mentally accept nothing but first class when it comes to your production, your brand, your presentation, your reputation - everything that's affiliated with you needs to be first class! With a first class mentality, you will then receive a first class perception and that's what you want. By having that mentality, it is going to

separate you from everyone else and that's the end goal - to be different! The way you present (market) yourself will determine your difference by an inch or by a mile.

The first class mentality will save you in situations where you think something is not possible. It proves to your mind that if you actually put in a tiny bit more effort right now, you can achieve what it is that you want.

The first class mentality is easily implemented - all you have to do is to go the extra mile in whatever it is that you do. Whether it's washing your car, making a sale, making a meal, cleaning your room, setting goals, helping someone out or simply just achieving a target. And what individuals in society primarily suffer with is laziness! And the decision to be lazy or not is all in your control! (Body and Mind).

Product Differentiation

Providing a different product or service is what the market buys. Have you noticed that whenever a new burger comes out at McDonalds, the market gets excited and they want to jump on it to try it out? Why? Because it's NEW and DIFFERENT and that's what you need to become. New and different - You can't be just the same old average Joe? That won't lead to you standing out and becoming an icon!

Be different in whatever it is that you do. Have the confidence to move forward and do the things that other people are not willing to do.

A great example of this concept was when I first started working at the Australian Stock Report. When I first started working there as a sales representative selling stock picks subscriptions, I started with another 5 trainees. We all got recruited the same day, a week had passed into the role and 3 out of the 5 of us had closed a deal, however, myself and another rep had not closed a deal. It was Tuesday at 11 am, my manager came up to him and I and pulled us aside – once this happened I knew it wasn't good news. He said to us "guys, unfortunately, this is a business and we look for an ROI on each of the sales reps we bring on board. If both you guys don't close a deal by Friday, I am letting you go". I took that information to my heart and I guaranteed that I was going to do anything in my possible power to assure that I close a deal because this was my position and I was going to keep it. That day, I did not take a lunch break, I stayed in the office until 10pm that night, making call after call after call after call. I lived 1 hour away from the city that time, and my position was in the city, so I arrived home that night just after 11 pm. When I woke up the next morning, I was the first one in the office at 7 am. I jumped on the phones and was calling clientele in New Zealand (Time difference was 2 hours ahead of Sydney time). Once again, I didn't take a break that day. I was the first in the office that day and the last in the office that night and come Thursday, I did the exact same thing. Friday came, my manager came up to the both of us and notified us that we both will be gone by the end of the day if nothing happens. That day, my colleague lost his job, I ended up closing 3 deals and became the bestseller for the week and every week and month after that!

Why? Because I was willing to do what other people were NOT willing to do. I didn't consider work as a 9 to 5 thing. I considered it a lifestyle and I made it nothing but my be all and end all to get this job done. The the only way to do it was to implement the first class mentality, refuse to accept no as an answer and demanded that through my actions, I will succeed.

Networking

Networking is so important in all of our lives. You need to do one thing and that's expose yourself. Whatever industry it is that you are in, you need to gain exposure right now. You need to attend and join each and every seminar/workshop/event/online group/webinar that your industry has to offer. The more exposure you get from the market, the more result the market will give you. You need to expose yourself and meet people who you currently don't know today and this can be applied literally in any situation. Whether you're an entrepreneur wanting to grow your business or whether you're a school leaver attempting to find a job or whether you're a current business person attempting to gain more market share. EXPOSING yourself further gives the market an understanding of who you are. If the market doesn't know you, it's not the market's fault, that's your fault.

You don't know who you will see or come across in any situation or scenario. The way life operates on a day to day basis is in your control - but it is only in control by you leveraging off all opportunities available. Therefore exposing yourself is key! Now, I want you to think about this concept for a second.

Why is it at school whenever we had an assignment or a task, we would go to the 'nerds' for the answers? WHY? Because they had the answer right? Well now that we are aware of it, we need to maintain relationships with the right individuals or the so-called **NERDS** of that industry and use that person or persons and LEVERAGE off their expertise to grow ourselves.

Through networking, you gain the following:

Relationships

Relationships in life and in business are vital. You need to consistently grow yourself by surrounding yourself with the right people and that all starts by building and starting new relationships. New relationships provide you access to new perspectives, new outlooks and new experiences that you can use in your life!

Fresh ideas

Networking gives you access to fresh ideas. Think about it this way - let's say for example tonight you were heading off to an entrepreneurship event or a business event. Wouldn't you agree that you're going to meet a bunch of new people? Wouldn't you agree that not only the speakers at the event are going to give you fresh new ideas because you will be watching them and learning, but amongst the crowd, while networking and meeting new people, you will be discovering new ideas along the way which are going to assist you in growing as a person and a business!

New Information

By networking, you will be speaking to people who are learning how to do it or even people who have done it already. This will teach you how to grow yourself or business. This will teach you different methods on how to tackle the market, you will be exposed to new information, new processes, new methods which you can implement in your business. No one is perfect and we can consistently learn and grow as humans, but if you are not willing to take action and grow yourself by learning, you will stay in the exact same position that you are in today.

Advice and support

Perspectives are perfect, especially from the right people. Networking with the right individuals will give you the most accurate advice that you need. By presenting your ideas and working with other people in the marketplace who have done it before, you can gain a better insight on how to grow yourself or your business. Perhaps you could build or establish a relationship that you never once had because someone that has seen what you have to offer wants to work alongside you and support your growth because they also believe in what you have to offer. Just consistently work towards growing yourself and the right advice will come, but chase it.

Exercise

How do you feel your consumer perception is, in the marketplace?
....
....
....
....
....
....
....

What reputation do you want to send out there for yourself and what change are you going to make as of date to get that status?
....
....
....
....

IV) Accounting & Finance

Money. That word. It's funny how far you can get in this world if you simply have a lot of it. However, if money isn't managed, you'll forever be in a situation that will not benefit you financially. Money I believe is the international language that the world speaks. In this world, you can build whatever you want, own what you want (materialistic that is), only if you have money. It can be yours, however, the low and middle class will stay where they are and nothing will change in their lives if members of those classes don't implement some form of management towards their finances.

Your perspective towards money, in general, needs to change, for the outcome to change. This needs to be drilled into your paradigm;

"Money is an object, move it around to benefit you, don't rely on it"

- Patrick Osman

What I've found pretty common is the bill chase. Where people work week to week, paycheck to paycheck & get stuck in this cycle.

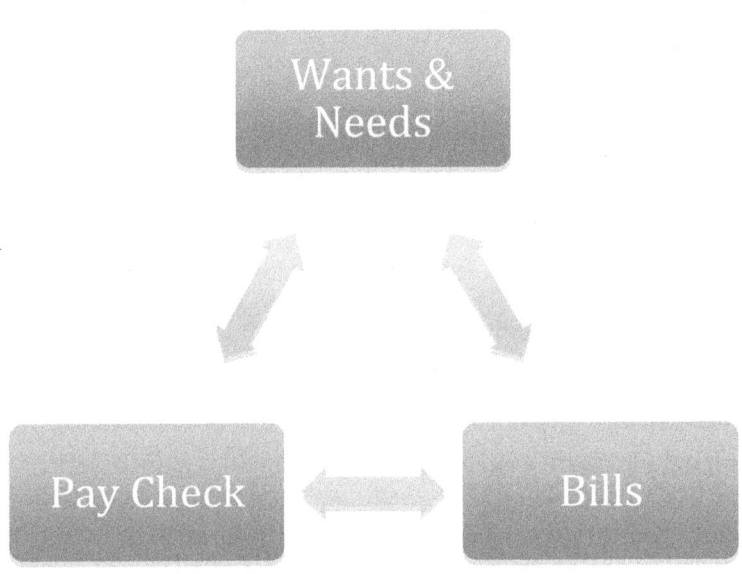

These elements; Pay-Check, Bills, Wants & Needs - this pattern need to be altered to benefit you in the long run. What happens, is that because people don't have a specific desire or goal in their life, they are then driven by paying their bills and their basic wants and needs, opposed to being driven by their goals. If this is you, you need to address your current financial situation. Your perspective towards money needs to change immediately. Simple strategies you can implement to increase financial efficiency in your life:

- Create more paychecks (creating more income streams)

- Decrease bills/expenses (to satisfy literally what you only NEED to pay for)

- Wants and needs need to be altered (to what you mathematically can afford. Dinners, outings with friends all need to be minimized until you can afford it. Stop living the lifestyle that you think you can afford up until you can afford it!)

Money comes in numbers and with simple mathematics, your financial position can be forecasted. If you know what you regularly receive, anything else that you receive on the side from any side hustles, you shouldn't even have access to, that needs to go straight into savings with the intention of future investment. The difference that you will receive from the increase in paychecks + decrease in bills + decrease in wants and needs is a number. That number should then go towards a savings account that is going to contribute towards an investment - whether it be a business idea or real estate.

Investing in yourself

Your mind is your greatest asset that you own. Money should consistently be going towards investing back into yourself - you need to be investing into your brain. Knowledge is power, the world knows that. Without knowledge, you cannot move forward and excel in your business or in your life. Irrespective of the price, if it's a book, workshop, seminar, course or whatever educational event it is. The return on the investment will be a positive return, either way, putting aside the networking opportunity and the exposure that you can generate from simply just attending the event.

"An investment in knowledge pays the best interest" - Benjamin Franklin

The more knowledge you put into your brain, the more you differentiate yourself as a product. Just knowing more about whatever it is that you're dealing with will give you an immediate advantage in the marketplace. If you're in sales, make it your goal to read 2 sales books a month, watch a sales training video daily and attend a couple sales training seminars that year. Be willing to travel and expose yourself, this is where your money should be going back into - back into yourself, back into your brain, back into growing you, becoming a better version of you. Money comes to all of us, but how we deal with it will determine where we can be tomorrow.

Creating Income Streams

This is the way that I see it; there are some people who wake up every day go to work, come back home and watch some television or go to the gym, have some dinner then sleep. The next day is repeated and the next day is repeated and so forth. Now, I want you to think of things a tiny bit differently here. The way I look at it (Pat's perspective); Wake up every day, leave your house, get into the marketplace, go and find where your money is located, who has it, find who you have to take it off, bring it back home, bank it, go out the next day and do the exact same thing. If you have a salary capped at $90,000 or $100,000, whatever it is that you earn, one thing I have to say to you is that you have the opportunity to make a lot more than that because time gives you that opportunity. Moreover, what happens is that one usually mentally caps and limits their financial position based on their ONE paycheck. It's now time to raise the bar and increase the amount of revenue that comes into your life.

You are a business, now you need to stop and think that whoever you work for is a customer. Wherever you generate any form of income from, consider that avenue of cash a client. Your main form of income from your prime position (full time job or business), consider that your largest paying client, however, now you need to pick up more clientele (more income streams) because you need a lot more cash coming through the doors. Therefore, more clientele means a second job, earning a second contract or an investment in another business or property providing you with a positive return.

Ultimately, what you want to do is treat yourself like a third party and have your investments provide you with your weekly or monthly paychecks. Refer to the following model that explains how your cash should be ultimately flowing:

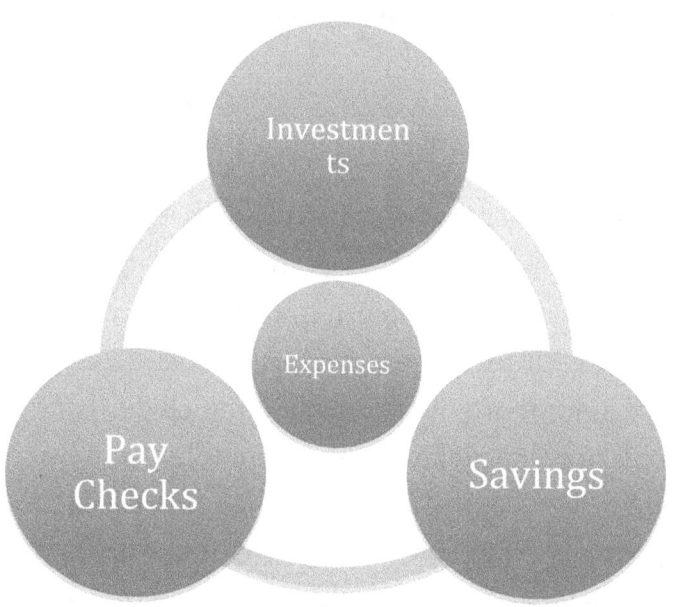

The ultimate goal is to have multiple income streams flowing into your life so that your income collectively outweighs your expenses. Increase your paychecks. You need to have money coming into your life from different angles and you can do that through leveraging off two components in your life which are: internet & free time. In today's society, with the use of the Internet and specific websites like Fiverr, Zeerk and Gigbucks provide additional income streams for everyone worldwide. You can provide any form of service that people are looking for in return for some quick cash! How awesome is that? This is a tiny example of how you could increase your cash flow. If you duplicate your efforts and implement the first class mentality in what it is that you want to excel in, you will differentiate yourself and earn a lot more business.

Whenever you have free time, I want you to stop and think, 'is what I am doing right now providing me with a return on my investment?" At the moment I'm investing my time into hanging out with friends, watching the basketball, playing games or even heading out for a few drinks. There's nothing wrong with all of those things .. but what happens in society is that people abuse fun time and always end up in a financial deficit in their personal financial lives because they emotionally satisfy the short term. That's what you don't know. You need to be willing to risk your time now so that in a couple of years' time, you can be enjoying yourself on a much larger scale. Minimizing expenses and increasing income should always be in the back of your mind. If you come home after work one day, my question to you is, what are you doing from the hours of 7 pm – 1 am? What are you doing on Saturdays and Sundays? What are you creating? What services are you providing? Where are you working? Are you providing your life with an additional income? If you're not satisfied with your current wage, that means you DEFINITELY have the hours in a week to do something about it and make a lot more cash. Put the ego aside and go become a cleaner, flip burgers! Do anything possible to increase your cash flow. If it needs to be done, it needs to be done.

Business and emotions don't mix. It's funny to prove that point. I remember a while back, I was selling CCTV Surveillance systems and there was this one prospect - a nightclub. I kept on trying to cold call the owner throughout the week and I couldn't get through to him during the day. I even stepped into the business itself to attempt to meet him and he was never there. The doors were always closed throughout standard Monday to Friday work hours. 2 weeks went by and I couldn't handle it. I thought to myself, it's time to implement the first class mentality and do anything in my power to get ahold of this prospect (it wasn't even a guaranteed sale!). I then ducked out on a Sunday night, dressed up in my suit, drove 1 hour to Sydney's red light district, arrived at the nightclub and asked to speak with the owner. He walked out and looked at me with a puzzled face and abruptly asked me, what I was there for? I responded by saying that I was there to upgrade his CCTV surveillance system. He was shocked he said "What? Why are you here on a Sunday night" I responded by saying "Because sir, the couch doesn't pay me, you do." He smiled and with open arms, he invited me into his office. He appreciated my honesty and happily listened to my pitch and of course I didn't walk out of that room without his signature.

Once I had attempted to contact the prospect and couldn't get through, I decided to implement the first class mentality and of course, it didn't let me down.

Always understand that you can make more money. Whether you dedicate your weekends to committing to an additional side hustle, mobile car washing services, lawn mowing services, dog walking services - whatever it is, organize yourself to increase your income NOW!

Emotions and Finance

"If you cannot control your emotions, you cannot control your money" – Warren Buffet

Money doesn't have feelings and this is where you need to detach your feelings from your bank account. Over the next page, you'll see that I've configured a basic financial risk curve that's going to make you conscious of your spending habits:

Financial Risk Curve

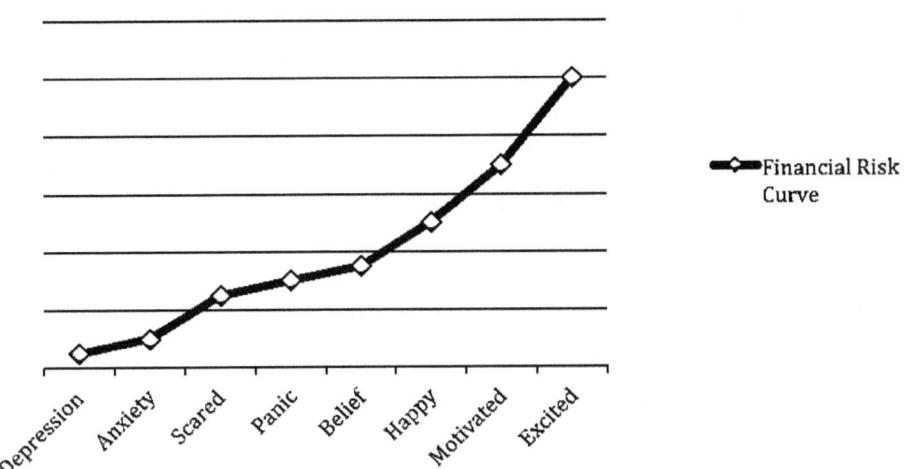

As you can see, the highest point of financial risk is when one is excited and the lowest point is when one is depressed. When you are in an excited mood, you've obviously made a decision that you're willing to move forward with and the dopamine has now kicked in and is giving you the energy to impatiently take action and take that step. This is where you have to be emotionally intelligent and stop your emotions from persuading you. Don't negotiate with your mind. Don't even listen to it! If you know that this next decision does not logically add up and provide you with a benefit for tomorrow, then don't move forward with it. You need to make sure that if you are not in a comfortable financial position, then every financial decision you make prior to you being at the right financial position, needs to have a return on investment. It needs to financially benefit you moving forward. Looking at the graph from the other side of the spectrum, you can see that when one is depressed, financial risk is low. Therefore your buying behavior is dramatically low. You lack the motivation to make a decision, let alone a financial decision. This is where you need to make sure that in the event you need to make a decision on behalf of your business or yourself, irrespective of if you feel the business is going to be at benefit, go ahead and do what it takes to assure that the needs are met. For example, paying a parking ticket. You are not happy when you pay it and the policeman pulls you over. But, in the event that you refuse to pay it, then things can go tremendously wrong - perhaps the bills could increase! You don't want to disturb your financial position further than its current situation. Own up to your mistakes, pay what you need to pay and move on. Whinging is for babies - you aren't a baby anymore. It's time to move forward. Pay your expenses and bills with confidence and complete your journey of conquering this Earth!

Your business doesn't care if your boyfriend or girlfriend broke up with you - it needs to be paid so then it can pay you. Once you get paid, your investments ultimately will turn to bringing you residual income every month - all from the single seed that you planted which went in your initial investment.

Return On Investment

In any situation where your funds have to leave your bank account, it's best to leave your emotions out of the decision and ask yourself "what is the return on my investment?"

If funds are leaving your account and going towards a car for example? It costs $50,000. It doesn't make you money. Yes, it can get you to work and back, but you could also use public transport to get you to and from work. Therefore there are alternative methods to get you to and from work. Primarily, it doesn't generate you income therefore, I would consider a car a liability. Is there that much of a return on your investment to outlay $50,000 of your own capital on a weak asset that is more of a liability? I don't think so. You're better off leasing the vehicle or buying a much more cost effective car at a tremendously lower price, say for example $10,000 and consider investing the additional $40,000 into an investment property or straight into the bank to keep it growing for a future investment that you have planned.

Exercise

Select 5 different times where you have spent money instead of invested money

....

....

....

....

....

....

....

....

....

....

....

....

....

....

Make Reference to the Financial Risk Curve. Explain a time where you made a poor financial decision based on your emotions that didn't provide you a with a ROI & how would you deal with that situation in the future?

Email: Patrick@patrickosman.com

Facebook: Patrick Osman

Youtube: Patrick Osman

Instagram: thepatrickosman

Snapchat: pattawesom

Twitter: thepatrickosman

CHAPTER 4

MANAGING RISK IN YOUR BUSINESS

Understanding that all functions are interdependent on each other - you need to remember that this is what's going to benefit you.

Preventing any business from internal risk should be one of any business's main priorities.

If you are conscious of this concept, you need to make sure that you protect your business from failure.

Here are some factors that could influence you in a negative way that you need to be cautious of, and also some additional tips that are going to get you a step ahead:

Friends

This is self-explanatory, friends talk to you every day. They converse with you about specific topics. Whatever it is that you cover in your conversations throughout your day to day activities with your friends ends up determining the way you think. If you are surrounding yourself with positive individuals then the way they think will be like a domino effect upon your brain and in turn, will be the way that you think! It's not either of our faults, it's our conscious mind. It processes any form of information that our senses have affiliation with, and if it is connected with that specific topic for over a 3 week period, then it will dump that information straight to our subconscious mind and the perspective of that specific topic will then be a part of your paradigm. That's simply how it works. If your friends are not supporting you in whatever business or career decisions you are making; if they are bringing you down instead of making you the person that you should become, they need to be fired. You are the CEO of your life and you need to recruit nothing but the best employees for your business. Don't forget that. Let's set things straight. You don't have time to sit around and watch the sky change from day to night - you have a career to create.

You have a life to build. You have future to look forward to. It's mandatory for you to be surrounding yourself with individuals who want to make it in life. Your friends need to be the ones by your side who are PUSHING you to succeed. You cannot be dwelling with ones who want to consistently be consumers. You need to surround yourself with individuals who want to become producers.

Instead of mass consuming, you need to mass produce.

"I am a success today because I had a friend who believed in me and I didn't have the heart to let him down"

- Abraham Lincoln

People's Advice

This one is quite funny. People love to be known as the expert. What you will notice throughout your career is that individuals who are not the correct and credible source will provide you with advice and most of the time it's negative or opposing, and that's wrong! So many dreams have been crushed by the wrong people. We all have dreams and wants in our lives and little do you know that the best person to give you advice is life. You need to experience things for yourself so don't allow people's perspectives to determine your life's direction. Allow your own experiences to determine your direction, however, seek the advice of the correct individuals when you need to. Whatever field it is that you are in, whether you're in sales, just seek an individual who understands how to persuade clientele and has been successful at it and make them your mentor. If you're wanting to start your own business, find a business person who you know for a fact knows how to run a successful business and speak to them. Get to know more about how they did it. Then duplicate the exact same mentality and procedure! At least you know for a fact you're getting information from the right person opposed to a clueless person who thinks they know what they're talking about.

"Your time is limited, so don't waste it living someone else's life. Don't be trapped by dogma – which is living with the results of other people's thinking. Don't let the noise of others' opinions drown out your inner voice. And most important, have the courage to follow your heart and intuition. They somehow already know what you truly want to become. Everything else is secondary"

- Steve Jobs

Family

Family is beautiful. The concept of the family should definitely be a part of your goals and always attempt to strengthen your relationships with each and every single one of your family members. Family sometimes can be ultra-supportive of your business or career decisions and other times they can be completely demotivating. Whatever happens, if you have made a decision for yourself and you know for a fact that it is the best decision for your career, irrespective of what your family says, stick to your goals and satisfy your vision. Family will put you down and it's not their fault. They probably don't think that what you want to do is the best for you, however, if it is genuinely what you want and you know for a fact that your intuition and soul are screaming to pursue that specific career, then DO IT! My family thought I was an absolute idiot - I mean I worked in every possible workplace. I changed my job at least 25 times! My dad at one point sat me down and spoke to me about my life and which direction I was heading. I told him that I was not going to give up, no matter who believed in me or not. I had aunties and uncles laughing at me because I didn't have a 'stable' career. I've heard it all from all different family members. They told me to just go back to university and get a good stable job at a bank. That didn't do it for me. I knew that my "why" and my purpose on planet Earth was not to sit down and take orders from people and get paid the minimum wage to do it. In life, you have one shot and you have to make sure that you get up and take action based on decisions that you want - don't live a life for others.

"Family,
They drive you crazy.
They drive you nuts.
They drive you loony.
But they are the only other human beings on this planet with the same blood as you"

- Patrick Osman

Social Media

Social media is something that needs to be used daily. The world can be accessed through a simple click of a button. Remember how much I spoke about the subconscious mind, right? You need to control what goes in and out of your brain. If you're not on social media for business purposes, you need to reduce the amount of time that you are on social media. Celebrity gossip won't get you far - it will only pay celebrities bills a lot more than yours. Remember that. You need to be a producer, not a consumer. At the moment, people are being consumed by the celebrity world and people follow celebrity lifestyles religiously like it's their own. Control what goes on your social media and don't allow any negativity to get into your brain, let alone in your visions way.

Just remember who's really benefiting at the end of the day.

"Face your problems, don't Facebook them"

- Unknown

Television & Radio

Negative. Don't even BOTHER with television and radio. The media throws consistent negativity your way whether on the news, radio or on television. I don't watch TV at all. I watch movies, sure, no downside there at all, but no way will I sit down and watch the news or watch television. Control what you watch. YouTube and podcasts have taken over now - get on YouTube and use YouTube to your advantage. You can select pretty much whatever you want to watch! Last time I checked there was over 819,000,000 hours' worth of videos on YouTube. Whatever topic it is that you want to learn from, it's waiting for you to view it. Use your time wisely. Educate yourself while others are watching other people get paid. Don't get me started on the negative focus that the news has.

Focus on yourself, get away from that screen.

"Why haven't you ever seen a Lamborghini commercial before?
Because the people who can afford them are not sitting around watching TV"

- Unknown

Time

See, a lot of people complain about their lives and claim that life is hard. The reason why they would claim that is because they have not adapted to their situation. Not only that, but they have not planned their life accordingly. If you are not aware that taking action is a large component towards success, then forever you will stay in that one position that you're currently stuck in. A lot of us don't move forward in life and fulfil our dreams because our subconscious mind controls us without us knowing. What happens is, in our mind, we create limitations and belief restrictions which then prevent us from moving forward and creating the life that we want. The end goal for all of us on planet Earth is to be happy. Ultimate happiness is the end goal.

Now understanding that there are 168 hours in a 7 day week, your sleep consists of an average of 49 hours for that week and work takes an average of 40 to 50 hours a week and the other 74 hours (roughly) would be considered your spare time. What are you doing in your spare time? Understanding the importance of time will give you an immediate step ahead of everyone else in the marketplace, starting off with something as little as the days of the week, right? Now here is where I'm going to provide you with a different approach to looking at life and it's funny because all it is, is a different perspective. However, once this perspective is understood, you will notice that you will become a lot more productive throughout the week with respect to having time on your hands. Now, the days of the week. Yes that's correct, the days of the week. let me ask you a question, have you heard of "TGIF"? (Thank God it's Friday) It's an internationally famous saying in which the world LOVES and shows gratitude to Fridays because of the weekend break.

Do you see that? The mind has screamed internationally and sent a message to the world saying that people can't wait for the weekend. Hold on. let me just register this. People are willing to work and allocate 40 to 50 hours of THEIR life in sacrifice for a weekend which is just 48 hours… Does that make sense? Clearly not. No way in hell!

What's happened is, society has generated a specific perception of each day of the week, i.e. Monday is devastating because everyone is back to work, so now automatically people are not in a positive mood on Sunday night and Monday morning. Wednesday is 'hump day' which is the middle day of the week and Saturday is the day in which one enjoys themselves by heading out for drinks on Saturday night etc. That whole perception needs to fly out the window NOW!

That whole perception is nothing but a consumer perception that clearly contributes to mass consumerism. The way I view life is simple, there's no days in the week. Each new day that I wake up to is just simply ANOTHER 24 hours. It's simple. When you view each and every new day as just another set of 24 hours, you will realize that the social perception of each day of the week will not influence the way you initially think that morning, and you will wake up and work that day towards your goals, irrespective of what day, time or month it is. Sunday is Monday and Tuesday is Friday to me - it's all the same. It's not the days of the week, it's time to live life. What a lot of humanity forgets is that some people don't have the opportunity that you have. Some people don't have the opportunity to even live life. Some people were formed as tiny microorganisms then didn't make it through their birth - BUT YOU DID! You're alive, you're living, you have the opportunity to live on planet Earth. So while you're here, don't be sold the same old story that society has attempted to persuade all of us with. You need to wake up every morning and work towards one specific goal and that is your purpose.

"Time is an illusion"

- Albert Einstein

The Voice

You talk to yourself every day, in your head and have conversations that are just constantly flowing and flowing and flowing. At the gym you must hear it a lot when you're training. You try to motivate yourself to push one more rep and your mind is having conversations with you, telling you it's enough, don't do it. It's the voice. This voice directs you and tells you where to go. We all have it. Watch out for it! It has murdered people's dreams because people have listened to it. It has lead people to very bad decisions. The fact that you are now conscious of this voice the one thing I have to say to you is don't negotiate with your mind. If you make a decision or if you receive an initial thought in your mind, regardless of the reasoning that pops into your head, go ahead with it. Listen to what your gut says. Ask yourself questions like, should I do this? And HOWEVER, you feel initially is what you should listen to. Not what the voice in your head says. Listen to how you feel! Go ahead with your intuition. It won't let you down. It can't let you down. It's advising your body to feel a certain way when that thought jumped into your mind, so the answer is there.

How it usually works is that initially you have an idea and after you have that idea in your mind, 'the voice' will then provide that idea with a negative argument which will attempt to persuade you. Don't confuse the negative argument with 'REALITY', don't fall into that trap. Believe in your initial idea and be stubborn about your ideas. Stick to them and listen to what your soul wants. Pursue it!

"If you hear a voice within you say 'you cannot paint' then by all means paint and that voice will be silenced"

- Vincent Van Gogh

Regret

Probably the worst feeling in the world? You can't get time back. No matter what happens, that's one element in life that you cannot get back, hence why I consistently stress that you use your time wisely and leverage off it! There are so many people that I have met in my life that have said these four words: "I wish I did!" Don't become that person - understand that those people are existing today. Right now you have the power and the time to not become that person. Take the risk, take the chance, take the required action and become the person who says: "I'm so happy that I took the chance". Because if you don't do it now, it's probably not going to happen. You have to breakthrough whatever mental battle it is that you're having and understand that if you don't take this chance or risk NOW and address your life, you will face the feeling of regret. It will hit you harder than any other feeling that life has to offer. Don't face regret, control it by taking action now. Don't let it win.

"Fear is temporary, regret is forever"
- Unknown

Just before you give up

Don't do it. There's no point. You've started for a reason. You got started on that one idea for a reason. Giving up is just wasting time. If whatever it is that you have decided to get involved in lies within your passion, if it's linked with your life purpose, then at some point, you're going to end up back on the same road that you were on when you started. The hardest part of your journey is the middle. The beginning is exciting. Everyone loves the beginning because you've just gotten started. You've mentally sold yourself the dream and you're ready to rock and roll. Throughout your journey you find the it very difficult. The business is getting no response from the market, people are not buying, you're losing money and so many other hurdles occur that you face along the way.

It doesn't matter how hard it gets, you made the

decision to get started in the first place. The cat can be skinned a thousand different ways so alter your methodology and change it so make sure you get what you want.

FIRST CLASS MENTALITY.

Implement it at all times.

"Don't cry to quit, cry to keep going"

- Eric Thomas

Be prepared

My mum always taught me that life is full of disappointments - that has stuck with me throughout my whole life. Whenever you start any venture or any new position, there are going to be some tough times ahead. These tough times are going to provide you with an experience that you have never experienced before. God has a written journey for us all and what we need to do as human beings on planet Earth, is to give life a shot and to live it. My saying is, as long as your heart does not stop beating, do it! Keep going through whatever issues come your way. Sometimes it can get really tough. You could potentially lose family members, you could be getting chased by the banks for debt, your assets could get taken off you. This will all lead your attitude to slump tremendously. I need you to stay motivated and understand that there will be some legitimate tough times. You are being warned! As an entrepreneur, there have been so many times where I can confidently tell you, I haven't had money to eat! I would be home alone, no money for food and I would go to my friend's house to spend time with them, but dude I was a hungry man! I needed to eat! I used to just eat there.

There have been countless times where I have been pulled over on the side of the road, in my suit, on the way to see clients and I had to reschedule my meetings because I didn't have money for fuel to put in my car.

My phone bill! My phones have been barred on numerous occasions! I've worked on commission only for most of my sales positions and if I didn't sell, I didn't get paid! That was tough, but I fought through the experience. As long as your heart doesn't stop beating, keep pushing through - there is a light at the end of every tunnel. Hard work will always pay. There will always be a return on your investment.

"Life is hard. And it isn't fair. And it really hurts like hell sometimes. But if you focus on what is within your power to change for the better, you can. And you will"

- Zero Dean

But what do they think of me?

This is a dream killer, a dream stopper!
One reason why I've come such a long way in my life at such a young age is because throughout my whole life, I have never once cared about what people thought about me. Obviously you want to make sure that you have a great reputation because 'consumer perception' is very important when it comes to succeeding in life. Sometimes when it comes to getting to where you want to go, people will perceive you as the person who is going to fail. They will tell you that you will fail and that you're a fool and they will call you every name under the sun. Only up until you are established is when you work on perfecting your consumer perception. Until then, focus solely on yourself and growing yourself to become that person that you've always wanted to become. You will be called many names along the way and people will put you down, but once they start putting you down, that's a sign that things are going well in your life.

Haters are fuel, leverage off it.

"One week they love me, next week they hate me. Both weeks I get paid"

- Grant Cardone

Keep your mind open

Your paradigm comes into play here. Initially, when it comes to anything that we have had an encounter with in our lives, we have a specific initial perception towards whatever it is. For example, some people feel that when they hit 30, their lives are over and it's far too late to start their career. They feel it's too late to go to university and graduate with a law degree because they feel that they won't get a job. Let's use another example - joining a network marketing company. People are immediately skeptical of the network marketing business model as a career, as it depends on growing your business through people like a pyramid. On the other hand, if someone was actually open to it and justified their initial reaction through whatever reason they find based on their due diligence, then there would actually be substance behind their decision opposed to being completely against it. What you need to do is to keep your mind open when it comes to making any decision and don't be so quick to judge. Because an open mind will give you access to experiences that you have never experienced before. Let me prove it to you. I want you to do something for me. Go look at a photo of yourself. Pick a specific photo and look at that photo and look at the person in that photo. The person you will be staring at in that photo is not the person reading this book. That person in the photo is the old you. You have evolved since then both physically and mentally. We are growing and evolving consistently with time. Go out there and gain experiences and plan the person that you want to be - prior to the next photo you take. Understand that your paradigm will answer for your brain majority of the time and now that you're conscious of being open minded, always think twice. Gain that experience and create a better future you.

"The mind is like a parachute, it only works when it's open"

- Unknown

Believe that it's going to happen

You need to believe in the unbelievable. Your goals need to be set so high that everyone thinks you're an idiot when you tell them your goals. What is the downside? Seriously? You need to aim freaking high man! In anything that you do, aim high! In the event that you don't achieve whatever it is that you're wanting to achieve, I guarantee you'll get close to it and getting close to your unbelievable goal or dream is better than setting a low target. Be crazy enough to think that you can accomplish anything because if you believe in yourself and swear by yourself, you will feel euphoric, which in turn will give you the confidence to conquer any task.

One of my favorite quotes of all time is by Steve Jobs, where he says "Because the people who are crazy enough to think they can change the world are the ones who do". I believe in myself so much, I just don't know any other way. I don't doubt myself one bit before I wrote this book as I knew for a fact that this is going to be an international best seller. I close my eyes and envision everything in my mind. I see me speaking to thousands of people and motivating them. I see me building churches worldwide. I see me motivating and inspiring people worldwide. Right this second, I'm sitting in my lounge room writing this book but at the same time, what's happening in my mind is what is important and what's happening is that I can see this book going worldwide. I'm believing in myself. I'm believing in the fact that this book is going to get into everyone's hands just like it's in yours right now. If I didn't believe in myself and gave up earlier, then you wouldn't be reading this right now. So believe in the unbelievable. You're a random human being that got put on planet Earth, that's floating in a solar system, in the middle of a galaxy, surrounded by millions of other galaxies. For God's sake, get up and do whatever it is that you want! Set your goals so freaking high that they are impossible and start making shit happen.

I believe in you. You should believe in you too.

Email me at Patrick@patrickosman.com if you have issues along the way, I'm here to help you.

"If you think you can or you think you can't, you're right"

- Henry Ford

Hunter for problems

Problems make people better people. If a baby didn't fall so many times before he or she started walking, then that kid wouldn't know how to walk. Problems provide you with experiences that teach you and make you aware of how not to do something.

It's quite funny, because Thomas Edison (inventor of the light bulb) said, "I haven't failed, I've just found 10,000 ways that won't work". There have been so many times where I've tried different methods of closing prospects, but I tried them because I wanted to know, which ones are the ones don't work so I can specifically focus on the ones that work! Whenever I would hire sales reps at the broking firm I was managing, the first day on the phones would be the most fun day for any new rep. Why? Because first thing I said to them in the morning is to enjoy today because I want you to try and get 300 people to say no to you before lunch time. And it was really easy. They were cold calling and pitching expecting people to say no. Of course, they would attempt to object handle each and every single prospect however, they needed to get 300 no's before lunch time. Half of them would be closing deals by 10am. You need to look for problems, go out and find them! Throw yourself in sticky situations, uncomfortable situations, crack out of your comfort zone and go and see problems! Get to Murphy's Law before Murphy's Law gets to you! When you hunt for problems now in the early stages, you are potentially eliminating future issues that may come your way because you are learning how to tackle these issues a long time before they do come. In the event that they do come in the future, you will handle them confidently and tackle the issue with no drama.

"We cannot solve our problems with the same thinking we used when we created them."

- Albert Einstein

Don't take No for an answer

The word no from now on should not make sense to you. It's time to become a yes man. When someone says no to you, you need to be shocked when you hear it. The word 'no' limits people's lives. It's a small word with such a powerful effect! That word stops people from living life! Whatever happens in whatever situation it is that you're in, whether it be your family, your colleagues, your friends, your prospects and even yourself, don't take no for an answer! If you take no for an answer, you are restricting yourself immediately. Think like a child. When a child wants something, they hustle, they push, they demand, they cry, they annoy, they throw tantrums up until they get what they want. They are persistent. They don't know what negativity is. They are driven. They have drive in them. They are focused on that one thing that they want and they don't give up and take no for an answer until they get it. I mean, if you think about it logically, what is the upside of accepting the word no? There isn't a point! It's boring? There's no upside - Life is a challenge! Accept it and wake up every day with a freaking reason! Don't wake up every day like a deadbeat not knowing what to do in your life. For God's sake, I'm 24, it's Saturday night right now and it's 11:12pm. A lot of people my age are probably in clubs right now taking a shot of liquor. That's not what I want. There's no ROI in doing that. I'd rather be changing the world and I believe that I'm going to and that's what YOU have to believe. Push, push, push, push, push! Don't stop! Wake up and keep going. If you get sad, accept that your excuses will not benefit you! The only thing that will benefit you from a sad experience is the experience and the feeling. The experience will teach you not to do it again and the feeling will make you change your life because the worst is when you are feeling sad and you've had enough! Never take no for an answer. If you want something, wake up, get up, push yourself and do not stop up until you get it. Control your mind and give your soul what it wants.

"Don't take 'no' for an answer, never submit to failure. Do not be fobbed off with mere personal success or acceptance. You will make all kinds of mistakes, but as long as you are generous and true, and also fierce, you cannot hurt the world or events"

- Winston Churchill

Put it on the line and leap

Why not? Seriously, you are alive for a certain period of time. On planet Earth, you have a time limit. Your time is written. We know for a fact that the lifespan of a human being starts as a baby and finishes at some point throughout that human's existence. Whether it's

50, 70 or even 100 years old.

Let me ask you a few questions: How old are you? How long have you existed on planet Earth? However old you are, have you enjoyed your life? Have you enjoyed living as a human being on planet Earth? Do you wake up every morning and feel happy? If you responded negatively to any of those questions, then I think that the both of us know that it's time to make that decision to take a leap and start working towards a happy life. There's no point of doing what you are doing every day if you are not looking forward to the next day. At one point in your life, to make it in life and become that person you've always wanted to become, you need to take a leap. There needs to be one massive risk that you have to take in your life to get where you want to be.

I remember I took that leap two years ago! Once I hit the point where I thought 'enough is enough.' I was managing the Australian Stock Report and I got sent to another state to assure the consistent growth throughout the company. The director of the company then refused to pay for my dinner? I stopped for a second and thought.. Hold on? I assisted in making AT LEAST 1 million dollars in revenue for that company throughout a 3 month period and I don't deserve my dinner to be paid for? I'm out! I'm taking a leap! There was a period where I didn't even have money to eat! Banks were chasing me to pay my debts but I was pushed into a corner because I didn't have anything to provide to any of the companies chasing me to pay my bills. That then forced me to build relationships with other businesses. I then started subcontracting myself as a salesperson to generate some cash throughout the time that I was building my speaking business. In the end, I made it through and you will too. I want you to know that once you jump, you will face some seriously tough situations. It's going to hurt and there will be back to back dramas, but once you start seeing the light at the end of the tunnel, you will forever live a lifestyle that you will look forward to. Put whatever you have on the line and take that massive risk! You'll walk away with an unbelievable story that will do two things: inspire others and change your life.

Work Ethic

Work hard. Always be the hardest worker in any room that you step foot in. If you want to have the results that you dream of every day, then work hard. Working hard every day is exactly like an axe chipping away at a piece of wood - you will arrive at your destination, but you need to slice that wood daily to get to the all end goal.

I want you to look at celebrities as a perfect example. We sit back and enjoy the songs and the movies that they produce. They're multi-millionaires but look at how they spend their lives. They are literally working long hours every single day. They spend hours and days on set working to provide the globe with entertainment. That's why they have net worths of millions of dollars - they are providing an international solution for entertainment. They are providing us with entertainment but they exchange close to every day to provide us with the entertainment that they do. Work like a celebrity. Work hard. Remember my perception on time. There's no 9 to 5. It's all about when your eyes open every day, until they shut. What are you doing for the time that you are awake? Are you being productive? Are you working hard? Are you getting closer to what it is that you desire to do and to be on planet Earth? Do what other people are not willing to do. Be the first to arrive at work and be the last to leave. Grow your position at work by becoming an icon in the building. Let people know you for being that person who would just work! That person who consistently just wants to produce! Become the master of your field and do it by working hard.

"Work ethic is the most important component of being successful"

- Kliff Kingsbury

The mindset of a child

"Mum, I want that toy. MUMMMMM I WANT THAT TOY!!!" The child then cries and kicks and whinges and whines and uses the strategy of being ultra-ANNOYING to get what they want. I'll tell you what, it works. I'm not telling you to kick your clients and start crying in front of them! What I am saying is to persist just like a child - they don't give up. They are focused on what they want and they do anything in their power to get what they want, because they know the joy that is going to come after they get it. They come into the Earth as pure souls who don't know any better. They are gullible, vulnerable, tiny beings that believe anything. So be like a child - believe in anything! Believe in the impossible! Of course, you want to believe alongside being conscious of realistic consequences to whatever actions you take. But stretch your limits to have a mindset of infinite belief. You have no reason to object to that. Any reason that objects to that is what I call a narrow mind! Don't confuse reality with negativity. A lot of people do that. Just consistently be like a pure child who believes that Mickey Mouse is another existing being on planet

Earth and watch what you will achieve.

"Children close their ears to advice but open their eyes to example"

- Unknown

Imagination

Your imagination can take you to places where your body has never been but your mind can be…Allow your soul to gravitate to this place where it wants to go to achieve ultimate happiness. Jump on a plane. Jump on a train. Go for a walk. Expose your eyes to new things that they have never seen before and put these new icons that you come across on planet Earth in your imagination and let it grow make and become an individual with infinite imagination. Life is a journey and it's here to be experienced by you. Allow your imagination to go to places. Use your imagination to your advantage. Allow it to expand. Think about specific things that you want to do on Earth then listen to your imagination and physically go out there and provide your soul with what it desires.

Albert Einstein once said that "logic will get you from A to B. Imagination will take you everywhere." Do you you agree with him? Don't you want to go everywhere? Don't you want to explore what planet Earth has in store for you? It wants to give you a journey! So write your goals down every morning, keep communicating with the universe and allow it to be provided to you. Close your eyes and imagine what it is that you want from life, then listen to your imagination. It will reward you by taking you to the places that you could have never imagined.

"The man who has no imagination, has no wings"

- Muhammad Ali

People create publicity

You're probably thinking, hold on. What's this guy getting at here?
Allow me to share a quick story with you. Do you remember the famous singer Barbara Streisand? Well, one day a company had taken a photo of a specific location and her house was located in the photo. She didn't like the fact that her house was located in this specific shot. So she attempted to sue the company to ultimately have this photo removed from their system. Once the news had hit the media that Barbara is suing that specific company to remove the photo, 10,000 people immediately jumped on it and downloaded it online. Prior to her taking legal action, there had only been 6 people who downloaded the photo - two of which were her lawyers. So tell me what does that say? She brought it upon herself! People created massive publicity about this issue and the photo went viral! Because people talk - whether it's good or bad marketing - exposure is exposure. People will talk bad about you. That's just the way some people operate. You need to understand that now! But the truth is, if you know that your product is genuine and you are genuine, allow the haters to provide free marketing for you. It's funny that I brought this up actually because

once I remember I was at an engagement and I had a group of people who were staring at me. One of the members of that group then approached me and said "are you, Patrick Osman?" I responded with, "yes I am. I'm assuming you've seen me online?" That person responded affirmatively. He then said, "my friends and I were just talking about how you do motivational videos online. You don't get paid for it? what's the point of you doing it? Why don't you just get a normal job where you can get paid a lot?" I then responded by saying "because my motivational services are that good, you guys are at someone's engagement and you guys are talking about me. That's free marketing for me which is going to lead to me one day speaking at a convention with 10,000 people there paying $500 per head to see me. Do the math." Then the conversation turned back to him and asked him what he did for work and we started chatting about his work. But that story proves that people talk and you can't change it. Whether they talk bad or whether they talk good, they will notify other people about you and your services. The other people who then hear about you, will do their due diligence and find out who you really are and that's the golden nugget right there.

"Fake people talk about other people being fake. Real people worry about their business and nobody else's"

- Unknown

Don't get caught up – get started

Don't be the person who gets caught up and allows their brains to take them in circles. Before you want to start a task, make sure you start. The downside to people who like everything to be perfect is that they attempt to master or perfect a task prior to starting the task or starting the business. What happens then, is that you are consistently costing yourself opportunity. If you are looking at starting something or making a big decision, make the decision, just do it! Go in at 60 or 70% because the other 40 or 30% of perfection will come with time. The market will provide you with the feedback that you need to tweak whatever it is that you need to tweak. Just get started! Sometimes getting started is the hardest part. Starting something really can get difficult but the only reason why it does get difficult is because of our brains and the voice in our head. The voice in our head diverts our thoughts onto different tangents which distract us and leads us to other thoughts that we don't need to be at. We then use these thoughts to create other problems in our heads, hence why we just don't start. Ignore the voice, grab the idea and run with it.

I want you to imagine something right now in your head. Imagine a screw and a nut. When you attempt to take the nut off the screw, it's so hard because it's so tight! But once you spin it anti-clockwise with enough force, it will end up coming lose and it spins off really easy after that, right? Well think about that and apply the analogy to your life. Getting started is the hard part but just spin the bolt and you'll notice that everything else will naturally follow. Life will never come up to you, tap you on the shoulder and tell you that it's the right time. You as a human being need to beat your emotions and create the right time.

"The secret of getting ahead is getting started"

- Mark Twain

Exercise:

What has been holding you back from becoming that ultimate human you've always wanted to become?

....
....
....
....
....
....
....
....
....
....
....
....
....

....

List 10 qualities without going back and reading the pages that you learnt from this chapter:

....

....

....

....

....

....

....

....

....

....

....

....
....

How are you going to apply these qualities in your life?
....
....
....
....
....
....
....
....
....
....
....
....

Email: Patrick@patrickosman.com

Facebook: Patrick Osman

Youtube: Patrick Osman

Instagram: thepatrickosman

Snapchat: pattawesom

Twitter: thepatrickosman

FINAL MESSAGE

GO OUT THERE AND CHANGE THE WORLD

Thank you so much. It was an absolute honor to share my perspective on how one's life should operate. It's funny because you are a business, and this book has proved that you are. Now that you understand you are an actual CEO of your own entity, get out there! Finish this book, pick up another one and grow as a human. Become the person that you've always wanted to become, don't be afraid to do it! Contact me if you need help along the way (Patrick@patrickosman.com)

Do impossible things. Manage your emotions. Sell yourself. Expose yourself. Travel. See things - do things! Live life to its fullest. Don't use the same excuses as everyone else. You can generate methods of how to get whatever you want in life, it's possible. Just put in the hard work and do literally anything possible to achieve what it is that you're after. If you don't do it now, the both of us know that you're probably not going to do it. Give your soul what it desires. Get your mind to strategize and get your body to do the physical work to assure that your soul is satisfied. Be influenced by your imagination, not by your surroundings. This world is so large Go and find out how you can conquer it. Also, don't forget, focus on yourself and only yourself up until you're established because, at the end of the day, it's best that everyone 'minds their own business'.

www.ingramcontent.com/pod-product-compliance
Lightning Source LLC
Chambersburg PA
CBHW070028210526
45170CB00012B/377